100 Legendary Drum Fills

by Jason Prushko

C000157488

CD Contents

1	Fill 1	21	Fill 21	41	Fill 41	61	Fill 61	81	Fill 81
2	Fill 2	22	Fill 22	42	Fill 42	62	Fill 62	82	Fill 82
3	Fill 3	23	Fill 23	43	Fill 43	63	Fill 63	83	Fill 83
4	Fill 4	24	Fill 24	44	Fill 44	64	Fill 64	84	Fill 84
5	Fill 5	25	Fill 25	45	Fill 45	65	Fill 65	85	Fill 85
6	Fill 6	26	Fill 26	46	Fill 46	66	Fill 66	86	Fill 86
7	Fill 7	27	Fill 27	47	Fill 47	67	Fill 67	87	Fill 87
8	Fill 8	28	Fill 28	48	Fill 48	68	Fill 68	88	Fill 88
9	Fill 9	29	Fill 29	49	Fill 49	69	Fill 69	89	Fill 89
10	Fill 10	30	Fill 30	50	Fill 50	70	Fill 70	90	Fill 90
11	Fill 11	31	Fill 31	51	Fill 51	71	Fill 71	91	Fill 91
12	Fill 12	32	Fill 32	52	Fill 52	72	Fill 72	92	Fill 92
13	Fill 13	33	Fill 33	53	Fill 53	73	Fill 73	93	Fill 93
14	Fill 14	34	Fill 34	54	Fill 54	74	Fill 74	94	Fill 94
15	Fill 15	35	Fill 35	55	Fill 55	75	Fill 75	95	Fill 95
16	Fill 16	36	Fill 36	56	Fill 56	76	Fill 76	96	Fill 96
17	Fill 17	37	Fill 37	57	Fill 57	77	Fill 77	97	Fill 97
18	Fill 18	38	Fill 38	58	Fill 58	78	Fill 78	98	Fill 98
19	Fill 19	39	Fill 39	59	Fill 59	79	Fill 79	99	Fill 99 and Fill 100
20	Fill 20	40	Fill 40	60	Fill 60	80	Fill 80		

1 2 3 4 5 6 7 8 9 0

Visit us on the Web at www.melbay.com — E-mail us at email@melbay.com

Table of Contents

Introduction

    This book goes through the most legendary and useful drum fills in rock music. Step-by-step we will break down a variety of drum fills ranging from busy fills to syncopated fills using clever spacing. You will be presented with a great variety of fills, focusing on hand-to-feet fills, tom fills, broken-up beats into fills, filling in odd times, and using rudiments to create an endless pallet of creation when approaching a drum fill in rock music. Being able to think of "time" in any feel, be it quarter note, 8th note, 16th note, and triplet is very important in having a truly endless variety of fills. Combining that with endless ways of orchestrating those feels around the drum set is what this book will teach you. Starting with simple effective fills, this book will get increasingly challenging, but once you've finished you will have a great grasp of filling in a rock setting. The goal is to be able to play these fills slow and fast. The audio has all the fills played at 100 beats per minute so you can clearly hear what is going on in each fill. Feel free to play along and increase your tempos once you have a grasp of the examples.

Going Around the Drum Kit

Examples 1-20 will focus on going around the drum kit different ways, using both hands and feet combined to create a full-sounding fill. These styles of fills can be heard in bands such as Led Zeppelin, Aerosmith, Jimi Hendrix, The Who, and Nirvana.

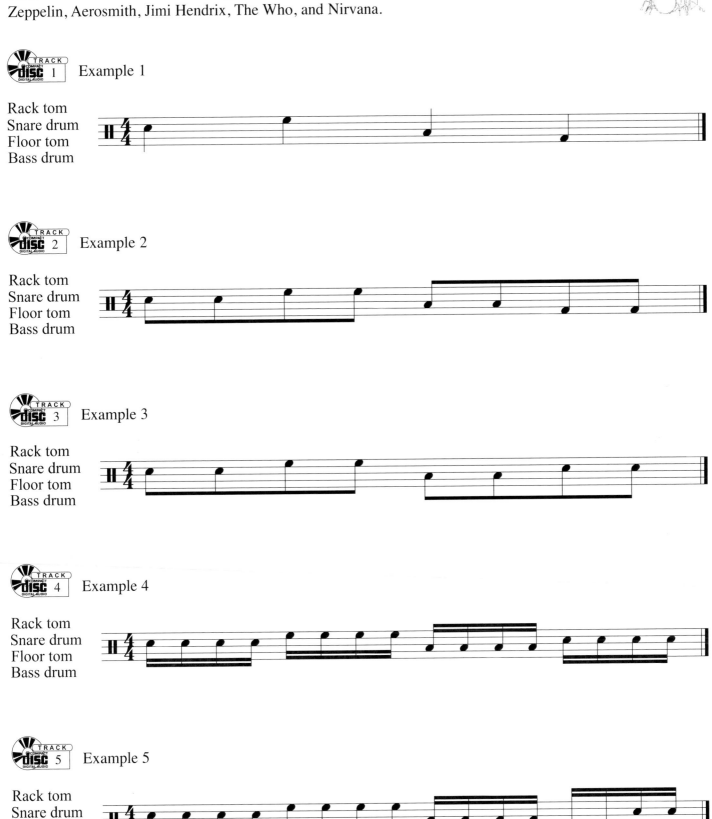

 Example 6

Rack tom
Snare drum
Floor tom
Bass drum

 Example 7

Rack tom
Snare drum
Floor tom
Bass drum

 Example 8

Rack tom
Snare drum
Floor tom
Bass drum

 Example 9

Rack tom
Snare drum
Floor tom
Bass drum

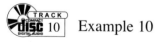 Example 10

Rack tom
Snare drum
Floor tom
Bass drum

Example 11

Hi-Hat
Rack tom
Snare drum
Floor tom
Bass drum

 Example 12

Rack tom
Snare drum
Floor tom
Bass drum

 Example 13

Rack tom
Snare drum
Floor tom
Bass drum

 Example 14

Rack tom
Snare drum
Floor tom
Bass drum

 Example 15

Rack tom
Snare drum
Floor tom
Bass drum

 Example 16

Rack tom
Snare drum
Floor tom
Bass drum

 Example 17

Rack tom
Snare drum
Floor tom
Bass drum

 Example 18

Rack tom
Snare drum
Floor tom
Bass drum

 Example 19

Hi-Hat
Snare drum
Floor tom
Bass drum

 Example 20

Rack tom
Snare drum
Floor tom
Bass drum

Hand-to-Foot Fills

Examples 21-40 will work on hand-to-foot fills, meaning we will break down cool bass drum to snare and tom fills, which played fast sound like a sweep around the drum set. Bands like Deftones, Led Zeppelin, Blink 182, The Police, and Return to Forever have made these types of fills legendary.

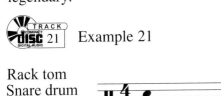 Example 21

Rack tom
Snare drum
Floor tom
Bass drum

Example 22

Rack tom
Snare drum
Floor tom
Bass drum

Example 23

Rack tom
Snare drum
Floor tom
Bass drum

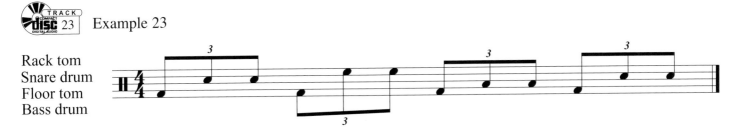

Example 24

Rack tom
Snare drum
Floor tom
Bass drum

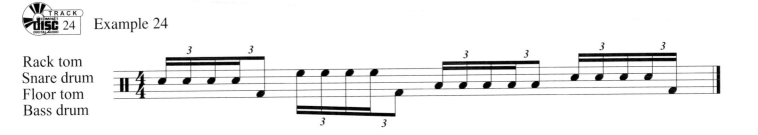

Example 25

Rack tom
Snare drum
Floor tom
Bass drum

Example 26

Rack tom
Snare drum
Floor tom
Bass drum

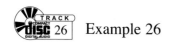 Example 27

Rack tom
Snare drum
Floor tom
Bass drum

 Example 28

Rack tom
Snare drum
Floor tom
Bass drum

 Example 29

Rack tom
Snare drum
Floor tom
Bass drum

 Example 30

Rack tom
Snare drum
Floor tom
Bass drum

Example 31

Rack tom
Snare drum
Floor tom
Bass drum

Example 32

Rack tom
Snare drum
Floor tom
Bass drum

Example 33

Rack tom
Snare drum
Floor tom
Bass drum

Example 34

Rack tom
Snare drum
Floor tom
Bass drum

Example 35

Rack tom
Snare drum
Floor tom
Bass drum

 Example 36

Rack tom
Snare drum
Floor tom
Bass drum

 Example 37

Rack tom
Snare drum
Floor tom
Bass drum

Example 38

Rack tom
Snare drum
Floor tom
Bass drum

 Example 39

Rack tom
Snare drum
Floor tom
Bass drum

 Example 40

Rack tom
Snare drum
Floor tom
Bass drum

Space in Fills

Examples 41-60 will focus on using space in your fills. Letting beats breathe is just as important as having massive "chops". Musicians like Jimi Hendrix, Frank Zappa, Incubus, Led Zeppelin, and Red Hot Chili Peppers are all great examples of groups using space when filling.

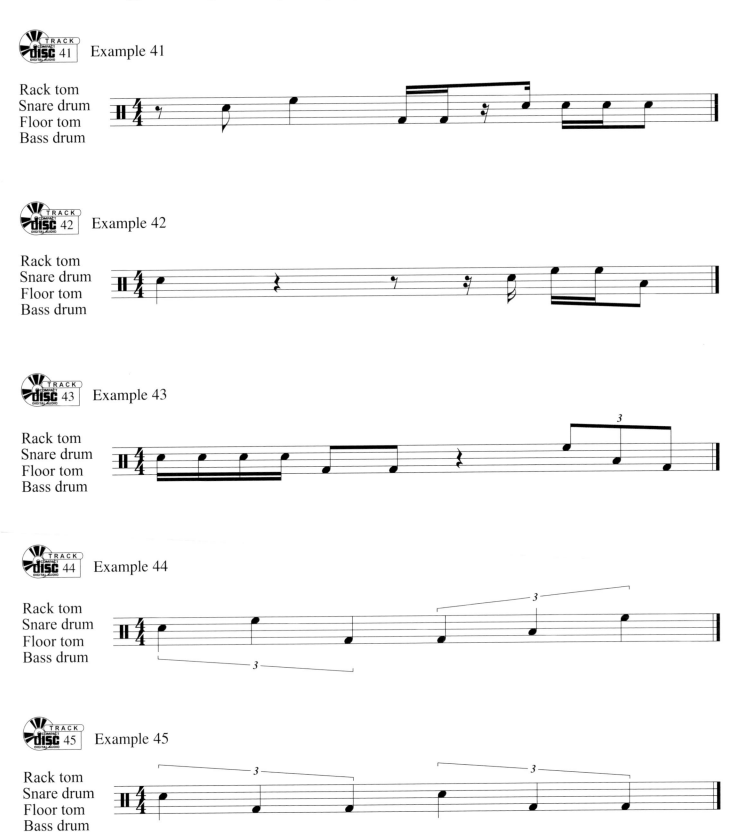

 Example 46

Rack tom
Snare drum
Floor tom
Bass drum

 Example 47

Rack tom
Snare drum
Floor tom
Bass drum

 Example 48

Rack tom
Snare drum
Floor tom
Bass drum

 Example 49

Rack tom
Snare drum
Floor tom
Bass drum

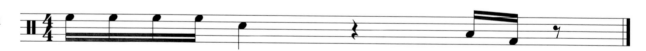

 Example 50

Rack tom
Snare drum
Floor tom
Bass drum

Example 51

Rack tom
Snare drum
Floor tom
Bass drum

 Example 52

Rack tom
Snare drum
Floor tom
Bass drum

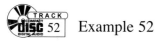 **Example 53**

Rack tom
Snare drum
Floor tom
Bass drum

 **Example 54**

Rack tom
Snare drum
Floor tom
Bass drum

 Example 55

Rack tom
Snare drum
Floor tom
Bass drum

13

 Example 56

Rack tom
Snare drum
Floor tom
Bass drum

 Example 57

Rack tom
Snare drum
Floor tom
Bass drum

 Example 58

Rack tom
Snare drum
Floor tom
Bass drum

 Example 59

Rack tom
Snare drum
Floor tom
Bass drum

Example 60

Rack tom
Snare drum
Floor tom
Bass drum

Broken-Up Beats as Fills

Examples 61-80 will work on using different broken-up beats as fills. Rudiments play a big part in this, so we will break down some different patterns and give you many options for making beat-like fills. You can hear great use of these techniques from bands like Dave Matthews Band, Tool, 311, No Doubt, and Box Car Racer.

 Example 61

Rack tom
Snare drum
Floor tom
Bass drum

 Example 62

Rack tom
Snare drum
Floor tom
Bass drum

 Example 63

Ride bell
Snare drum
Floor tom
Bass drum

 Example 64

Ride bell
Rack tom
Snare drum
Floor tom
Bass drum

 Example 65

Rack tom
Snare drum
Floor tom
Bass drum

 Example 66

Rack tom
Snare drum
Floor tom
Bass drum

 Example 67

Hi-Hat
Rack tom
Snare drum
Floor tom
Bass drum

 Example 68

Hi-Hat
Rack tom
Snare drum
Floor tom
Bass drum

 Example 69

Hi-Hat
Rack tom
Snare drum
Floor tom
Bass drum

 Example 70

Rack tom
Snare drum
Floor tom
Bass drum

 Example 71

Rack tom
Snare drum
Floor tom
Bass drum

 Example 72

Rack tom
Snare drum
Floor tom
Bass drum

 Example 73

Rack tom
Snare drum
Floor tom
Bass drum

 Example 74

Rack tom
Snare drum
Floor tom
Bass drum

 Example 75

Rack tom
Snare drum
Floor tom
Bass drum

Example 76

Rack tom
Snare drum
Floor tom
Bass drum

Example 77

Hi-Hat
Rack tom
Snare drum
Floor tom
Bass drum

Example 78

Hi-Hat
Rack tom
Snare drum
Floor tom
Bass drum

Example 79

Rack tom
Snare drum
Floor tom
Bass drum

Example 80

Rack tom
Snare drum
Floor tom
Bass drum

Odd Time Fills

Examples 81-100 will give insight to filling in odd time. We will go over fills with space as well as some busier fills. Bands like Rush, Dream Theater, The Mars Volta, and Tool all fill strongly in odd time. I play lots of odd time fills as well with my band, Mean Little Blanket

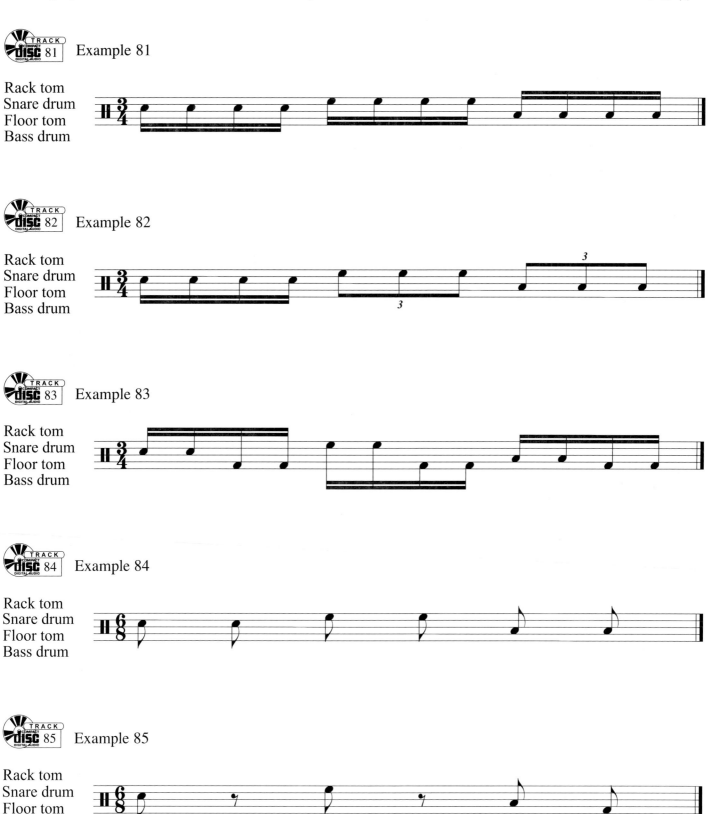

Example 86

Rack tom
Snare drum
Floor tom
Bass drum

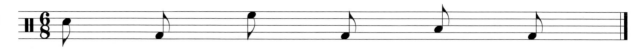

Example 87

Rack tom
Snare drum
Floor tom
Bass drum

Example 88

Rack tom
Snare drum
Floor tom
Bass drum

Example 89

Rack tom
Snare drum
Floor tom
Bass drum

Example 90

Rack tom
Snare drum
Floor tom
Bass drum

Example 91

Rack tom
Snare drum
Floor tom
Bass drum

 Example 92

Rack tom
Snare drum
Floor tom
Bass drum

 Example 93

Rack tom
Snare drum
Floor tom
Bass drum

 Example 94

Rack tom
Snare drum
Floor tom
Bass drum

 Example 95

Rack tom
Snare drum
Floor tom
Bass drum

 **Example 96**

Rack tom
Snare drum
Floor tom
Bass drum

 Example 97

Rack tom
Snare drum
Floor tom
Bass drum

 Example 98

Rack tom
Snare drum
Floor tom
Bass drum

 Example 99

Rack tom
Snare drum
Floor tom
Bass drum

 Example 100

Rack tom
Snare drum
Floor tom
Bass drum

About the Author

Jason Prushko is an American musician originally from Shelton, CT. He attended New School for Jazz & Contemporary Music (NY, NY), where he received a Bachelor's degree in Music Performance. Fluent in many styles of music, Jason performs in many settings. Jason is a freelance musician/session drummer, and has residency jazz gigs in Brooklyn, NY. Jason is also a co-founder and co-composer of American rock band Mean Little Blanket (www.meanlittleblanket.com), a hard-hitting rock band that is not afraid to take the listener through a wide spectrum of music. Jason also teaches private lessons and summer music programs in Bridgeport, CT.

The author's drum setup for Mean Little Blanket.